# TALES OF HORROR

# ZOMBIES

## Jim Pipe

**ticktock**

# TALES OF HORROR
# ZOMBIES

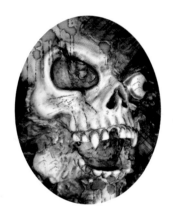

**Acknowledgements**

Copyright © 2006 *ticktock* Entertainment Ltd.

First published in Great Britain by ticktock Media Ltd.,

Unit 2, Orchard Business Centre, North Farm Road, Tunbridge Wells, Kent TN2 3XF, Great Britain.

All rights reserved. No part of this publication may be reproduced, stored in a retrieval system, or transmitted in any form or by
any means electronic, mechanical, photocopying, recording or otherwise, without prior written permission of the copyright owner.

A CIP catalogue record for this book is available from the British Library.

ISBN 1 84696 015 0 Printed in China.

Picture Credits:

t=top, b=bottom, c=centre, l=left, r=right, OFC=outside front cover, OBC=outside back cover.

Art Archive: 21b. Corbis: 8/9 (main pic), 17. The Kobal Collection: 4, 20-21 (main pic). Everett/ Rex Features: 5, 7b, 10tl. Rex Features: OFC. Shutterstock:
6tl, 7, 8, 9tr, 11, 13, 14b, 18tl, 19, 22/23 (main pic), 24/25 (main pic), 26tl, 30/31 (main pic), 31b. Superstock: 14/15(main pic).

ticktock Media image archive: 9, 14tl, 16b, 17t, 19 br, 27, 28b, 29, 29tr. Steve Truglia (prostunts.net): 13b.

Every effort has been made to trace the copyright holders and we apologize in advance for any unintentional ommissions.

We would be pleased to insert the appropriate acknowledgement in any subsequent edition of this publication.

# WHAT IS A ZOMBIE?

You hear moans, then shuffling feet. CRASH! An arm grabs at you through the window. CRUNCH! The door caves in. Zombies are on the hunt for your tasty, tasty brains!

A zombie is a dead person that has been brought back to life. It wanders about with its eyes staring straight ahead and its mouth wide open.

Zombies feed on humans. They love chomping on human brains. They often attack in big groups, ripping people into tiny pieces!

Zombies look like sleep-walking idiots, but they are strong enough to rip your body in half, or tear off your head.

The smallest scratch or bite from a zombie can turn you into one, too!

### THE FIRST ZOMBIES

Zombies first appeared in voodoo stories from Haiti, an island in the Caribbean. Voodoo is a religion from Africa. It came to Haiti in the 18th century, when people captured in Africa were taken to Haiti to work on farms as slaves.

Reports from Haiti describe the dead being brought back to life by voodoo sorcerers.

## TOXIC ZOMBIES

In the last 30 years, a new breed of zombies has appeared – toxic zombies! These creatures have rotting bodies covered in wriggling maggots.

Toxic means poisonous. Toxic zombies come to life when radiation or poisonous chemicals leak into the ground where they are buried. These zombies can't talk, they smell awful and have no fashion sense!

A zombie can feed at any time of the night or day. But toxic zombies are good night hunters. They can sniff fresh blood a mile away. They can also hear you breathing from the other side of the street. Keep very quiet if there are any toxic zombies about!

A toxic zombie has no sense of feeling, and lots of energy. Even if a zombie's body is badly injured, it just keeps on attacking. They can walk for miles and miles, but they don't jump and they don't swim. When hunting for victims, they stumble about rather than tracking them down. Luckily, a zombie only lives as long as it takes for its body to rot away.

### ZOMBIE LANGUAGE

Toxic zombies don't talk. They just moan. Their moans start as a rumble. They get louder and louder as they move into the attack. Then they rush at you with open jaws.

UUURRRRRGGGGGGG! This is one of the most terrifying sounds you will ever hear. The moan also tells other zombies that people are nearby.

# VOODOO ZOMBIES

I magine being given a drug that makes you look dead. When you wake up, you can see, hear and feel pain. But you can't control your body. You've become a voodoo zombie!

Voodoo zombies appear in stories from the Caribbean, Central and South America and the southern United States.

Voodoo sorcerers called houngans feed their victims with zombie powder. The powder makes the victims appear dead for up to two days. The voodoo zombies know what is happening around them, but they can't react.

After the person is buried, the houngan digs them up. They feed the victim more powder to make them stay a zombie. Then the houngan uses the voodoo zombie as a slave.

## BURIED ALIVE

There is a possible explanation for these stories about digging up zombies. In the past, doctors might have buried someone who was still alive (or in a coma), by mistake.

If grave robbers dug up their bodies to steal the jewellery that was buried with them, the people seemed to come back to life. But they were really just waking up!

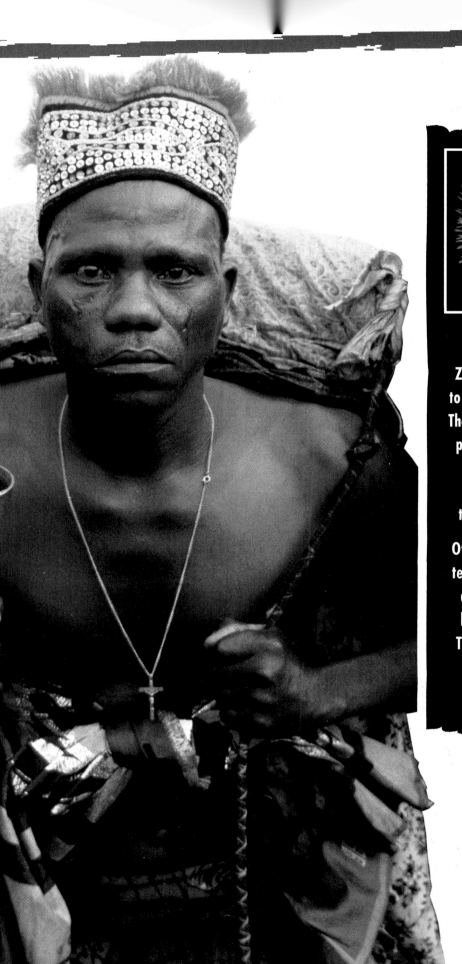

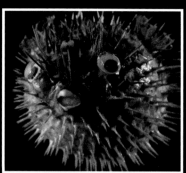

### ZOMBIE DRUGS

Zombie powder can be used to shut down a victim's brain. The powder can be made from poisons taken from animals such as the spiky puffer fish (above), the hyla tree frog or the cane toad.

Other voodoo zombie stories tell of people being forced to drink soup made from the leaves of the datura tree. The leaves contain a strong drug that is said to turn people into robots.

## ZOMBIE DO'S AND DONT'S

**Y**ou're alone in a dark, spooky house, miles from the nearest town. Outside zombies are gathering. Let's hope you packed well....

Here are some tips for staying alive if a gang of zombies are marching towards your house:

- Block off all doors and windows.
- Stay inside if you can and wait to be rescued.
- Gather food, water, torches, weapons and an emergency radio.
- Wear earplugs to cut out annoying zombie moans.
- Wear tight clothes so there is nothing for zombies to grab onto.
- Don't let zombies trap you in a corner.

If in doubt, run for it! You can move faster than a zombie. Make as little noise as possible and avoid open areas where you can be easily spotted!

### EVERY ZOMBIE FOR ITSELF

Sometimes just a few zombies attack. But as people are bitten they turn into zombies as well. The numbers grow bigger and bigger. Soon, thousands of zombies are on the attack, like a swarm of rats.

Luckily, zombies aren't smart enough to work as a team. If they were, we'd all be zombies!

# DESTROYING ZOMBIES

**W**ant to kill a zombie? Silver bullets won't work. Forget magic potions, spells or holy objects, such as crosses. In fact, there's only one way to kill a zombie. Chop off its head!

A zombie's skull is rock-hard. It's much easier to chop it off with an axe or a sword, than to crush it with a hammer or a sledgehammer.

Power tools might seem like a good idea. But chainsaws are heavy and you may chop off bits of yourself by accident.

When tracking zombies, watch for freshly eaten bodies. Hunting zombies takes a lot of guts. Work in teams and whatever weapon you use, don't let zombies get close enough to bite you.

Zombies are slow. So it is always better to run than stand and fight.

### ZOMBIE HUNTING

Running zombies over with a car works well. But you have to make sure you squash the zombie's head to kill it. Fire is no good because toxic zombies have no fear of fire. If they catch fire, they won't even notice it. A burning zombie becomes a living torch. It will set light to everything it touches, including you!

# VIKING DRAUGR

The word zombie has been around for about 200 years. It comes from the African word "nzambi", which means the soul of a dead person. But some zombie tales are thousands of years old.

### GRETTIR'S SAGA

"Grettir took all the treasure...but as he was making his way through the tomb he was grabbed by someone... they had a fierce struggle for a long time...but in the end the draugr fell backwards, and there was a great crash..."

This Viking story is over a 1000 years old. It tells how a Viking grave robber was attacked by a draugr, who wanted to hold onto its treasure!

### BLACK AS DEATH

A draugr was said to be "black as death". In some stories, a person killed by a draugr also turned black and became a zombie.

Draugr were incredibly strong. One story tells of a victim left "with his neck broken and every bone in his body crushed". Some could change into a cat that sat on a sleeping person's chest so they suffocated.

When the body of a Viking warrior was placed in its tomb, it came alive again. These Viking zombies were called draugr. Some draugr attacked the living. Other draugr stayed in their tombs, guarding their treasures.

A draugr had superhuman strength. Only a powerful hero could defeat it. Like a toxic zombie, a draugr was killed by cutting off its head.

In some legends the hero had to leap between the head and the body before the two parts hit the ground! The draugr's body was then burnt. The ashes were buried in a remote spot or thrown into the sea.

## GOLEMS

**W**ould you like a trained zombie to protect you from attack or do boring jobs around the house? Magicians in the Middle Ages did! They created zombie slaves from clay and mud.

In Jewish stories, brainless zombies were called golems. Jewish holy men called rabbis created them.

The golem was brought to life using the holy word 'Emet' which means 'truth'. This was written on the golem's forehead, or on a clay tablet put under its tongue. Golems could not speak or disobey their master.

In some stories the golem grew bigger and bigger. To stop the golem from hurting its friends as well as its enemies, the rabbi turned it back into dust by rubbing out the 'E' of Emet. This spells 'Met', which means 'death' in Hebrew, the Jewish language.

**THE LEGEND OF THE GOLEM OF PRAGUE**

In the 16th century a rabbi called the Maharal of Prague created a golem. He wanted to defend the Jewish people in Prague from racist attacks. The golem was made of clay from the banks of the Vltava or Moldau river.

As the golem grew bigger and bigger, he started killing people. The city council promised the rabbi that the violence against the Jews would stop. So the rabbi turned the golem back into dust.

## THE THINKING ZOMBIE

In the movie *The Fellowship of the Ring* (2001), the character of Lurtz is based on the golem legend.

Lurtz is a gruesome monster made from mud. He is brought to life by the evil sorcerer Saruman. Lurtz is different because he has a brain. He is a skilful fighter who leads an army of monsters. Lurtz is finally killed by having his head cut off – a classic zombie death!

# REVENANTS

**A**re you good? In the Middle Ages, people believed that anyone who had led a wicked life would rise from their grave to haunt the living.

In the Middle Ages, zombies were called revenants. They were blamed for spreading disease.

In some countries, people tied up the arms and legs of a dead body to stop it becoming a revenant. Sometimes the mouth was sewn up.

In some legends, a powerful wizard brings the body of a dead hero to life to carry out a dangerous mission. This revenant would be just as clever as he was in life. But he would be controlled by the wizard.

## THE LIVING DEAD

"The zombies appeared at evening, carrying on their shoulders the wooden coffins in which they had been buried... The villagers became sick and started dying. The bodies of the zombies were dug up... the heads cut off... this put an end to the spread of the sickness."

An account of the living dead, written by the Abbot of Burton around 1090 AD.

## SKELETON ZOMBIES

In the ancient Greek story of Jason and the Argonauts Jason and his men battle with zombie skeleton warriors. In one version of the story, Jason jumps into the sea. The skeletons follow but sink to the bottom!

This trick works on toxic zombies, too. If you swim across a lake, a toxic zombie will follow you, but it will soon sink to the bottom.

## MUMMIES

A mummy walks towards its victims, its arms outstretched. Its ancient, crumbling body held together by bandages. Run for your life!

In the movie, *The Mummy* (1999), the ancient Egyptian priest Imhotep falls in love with the king's wife. Imhotep is buried alive for 3,000 years as a punishment. A group of archeologists accidentally bring Imhotep's mummy back to life. The mummy goes on a killing spree. He uses his victims' bodies to rebuild his own rotting body.

Mummy stories may come from an ancient Egyptian myth. The god Osiris was killed by his brother Seth. His body was cut up by Seth and the pieces were scattered across Egypt. However, Osiris's wife Isis tied the bloody bits together with bandages and Osiris came back to life.

In the past, people thought mummies were magical. Many mummies were the dead bodies of ancient kings and queens. King Charles II rubbed ground-up mummy on his skin so that the "ancient greatness" would rub off on him!

## NOT A ROTTER!

The ancient Egyptians believed that a person's soul could not pass into the afterlife if their body had rotted away. Skilled workers prepared the body for burial. They removed the heart and pulled the brain out through the nose using a long hook! Then they dried the body with special salt and wrapped it in bandages.

Mummies had their arms tied to their bodies, and their feet wrapped together. So if a mummy did come to life it would hop, not walk! Mummies are also found in China, Japan, Peru and Egypt.

## CHINESE HOPPING CORPSES

China has its very own zombie, the hopping corpse. This zombie will stop at nothing until it has chomped on your neck. Some will choke you while you sleep. Sweet dreams!

Jiangshi, or "stiff corpses", feed on people to take their life force. But why do they hop? When a person dies, their body goes all stiff. This is called rigor mortis. These zombies stay a bit stiff, so they can only hop!

Hopping corpses are very easy to spot. They usually wear burial clothes from the time of the Chinese Qing rulers (1644-1911). These clothes went out of fashion hundreds of years ago.

Some have black tongues that hang down to their chest. Others have eyeballs that hang from their sockets.

And they stink! Some hopping zombies smell so bad a single whiff will knock you out!

### MOON ENERGY

Hopping corpses come to life using energy from the moon.

These zombies first appear in a myth called 'The Corpses who Travel a Thousand Miles'. In this story, priests use magic spells to move corpses over long distances. They get them to hop back to their hometown for a proper burial.

## HOPPING CORPSE PROTECTION ADVICE

• Don't breathe. The corpses hunt the living by smelling their breath.

• Piles of sticky rice stop hopping corpses moving.

• Burn the corpse to ashes, coffin and all.

• Some priests suggest nailing a piece of wood,
  about 15 cm high, across the bottom of your front door.
  Perhaps this stops zombies hopping into your house!

## GHOULS

These thin-faced zombies with bulging yellow eyes hang about in Arabian graveyards. They carry sleepy travellers into the desert, then tear them apart with their large claws and teeth!

A ghoul has a huge mouth that is lined with rows of tiny razor-sharp teeth. It has long arms and short legs. Don't look at it too hard because it often appears naked. A toxic zombie only eats living people. But a ghoul loves human flesh so much it eats dead bodies too.

A ghoul's home is usually an underground tomb or crypt. The sun's rays make it weak, so it only goes looking for meat at night. It sees well at night, and can smell human flesh (alive or dead) up to a mile away.

### THE BOGEYMAN

In Europe and North America there is a famous ghoul known as "the bogeyman." It enjoys hiding under beds or in cupboards in the dark. It waits until you are asleep then leaps out on you.

However, it only does this to scare you and is not that dangerous. The name bogeyman may come from the words "boggy man". Ancient bodies buried in peat bogs on moors were called "bog men". In the past, people were afraid that the bog men would come walking off the moors, like zombies!

# FRANKENSTEIN

**A** giant man walks stiffly towards you. Ugly, square face. Bolts through the neck. Stitches all over his body. Uh-oh! It's Frankenstein's monster.

The author Mary Shelley created one of the most famous zombie-like monsters of all time in her book *Frankenstein* (1818).

Scientist Victor Frankenstein creates a monster in his laboratory from the body parts of several dead people. He sews the body bits together and uses electricity to bring the monster to life.

However, the monster is not a mindless zombie. He is clever and knows how he was created. He feels emotions and pain.

After killing Frankenstein's brother, the monster hides in the mountains. He gets lonely, and asks Frankenstein to create a female monster to be his wife. Frankenstein does this, but then changes his mind. He destroys the female monster. This makes the monster so angry he kills Victor's father and wife.

## IT'S ALIVE!

"It was on a dreary night of November... I collected the instruments of life around me, that I might infuse a spark of being into the lifeless thing... It was already one in the morning... and my candle was nearly burnt out, when... I saw the dull yellow eye of the creature open; it breathed hard, and moved its limbs."

From *Frankenstein* (1818) by Mary Shelley.

# ON THE SCREEN

**Z**ombies are everywhere! From the TV show *Buffy the Vampire Slayer*, to the walking dead that terrorise London in *Shaun of the Dead*.

Shaun has a dead-end job and his life is going nowhere. But then the flesh-hungry living-dead start to appear in London. Shaun is forced to become a modern-day hero to save his girlfriend, his best mates and his mum!

In the first movie to use the word zombie, *White Zombie* (1932), a factory owner uses walking corpses as slaves.

*Night of the Living Dead* (1968), was the first movie to show the toxic zombies we know today. The zombies were brought to life by radiation from a space rocket.

Since then, zombies have appeared in countless movies. Special effects are used to show their rotting bodies and bloody attacks on humans.

## ZOMBIE INVASIONS

Movies give all sorts of reasons for zombie outbreaks. In *Plan 9 from Outer Space* (1959), aliens bring dead humans back to life. They plan to use this army of zombies to take over the world.

A common movie plot is a plague that turns people into zombies. A small group of survivors have to find a way to survive and stop the plague.

## COMPUTER ZOMBIES

Many computer games feature zombies as enemies. In the game *Zombies Ate My Neighbors*, the object of the game is to save your neighbours from being chomped up by zombies. In the game *Resident Evil*, scientists turn into zombies after a virus escapes from a secret government laboratory. *Resident Evil* has also been made into two movies.

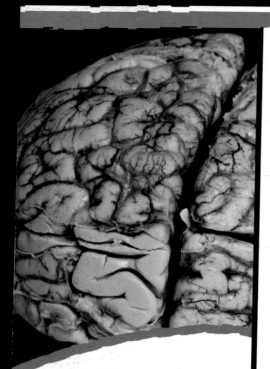

# DO ZOMBIES EXIST?

In 1937, people in a village in Haiti reported that they had seen a woman called Felicia Felix-Mentor wandering around the village. She had been dead and buried for 30 years!

In 1980, a man appeared in a village in Haiti. He said he was Clairvius Narcisse, who had died in 1962. Narcisse said that poisons had made him seem dead. He had even seen the doctor cover his face with a sheet. Narcisse claimed that a sorcerer had brought him back to life and made him into a zombie.

Could these stories be true? Maybe. We know about some powerful poisons that can make a person look dead for several days. The victim continues to see and hear but can't move. Perhaps other poisons exist that can make someone seem dead, for years!

Still, strange poisons do not explain where crazy, brain-eating zombies come from!

**Afterlife** Where you go after you die.

**Bog men** Dead bodies that are thousands of years old. They have been preserved in marshy ground.

**Coma** Being deeply unconscious for a long time. A coma can be caused by an injury, an illness or drugs.

**Golem** A brainless zombie slave from Jewish stories. Golems were created by Jewish holy men, called rabbis. They were made from clay and mud. Having a golem slave was a sign of great holiness and wisdom.

**Houngan** A voodoo priest, usually from Haiti. Houngans can turn people into zombies.

**Radiation** Energy that is transmitted in waves or particles. Radiation can take the form of electromagnetic waves, such as heat, light, X-rays, or gamma rays.

**Revenants** Zombies from the Middle Ages. It was thought that they were people who had been wicked in their lives.

**Vikings** People from Norway, Denmark and Sweden who lived about 1000 years ago. The Vikings were bloodthirsty warriors who explored Europe, Greenland and parts of North America by sea and land.

**Voodoo** A religion that began in West Africa. Today, it is mainly practised in Haiti in Central America. Voodoo followers believe they can contact their dead ancestors while they are in a trance.